and under following ISBN: 978-1-365-87919-7

MY MOVE

By: Leif Wilhelm

"The one who walks here in - there are no hope left fore.."

Quote: from Dantes: Inferno

G R A N D F I N A L E:

"IF ANYBODY SHOULD TRY TO CAPTURE ME!"

By: Leif Wilhelm the 1st of December 2003

"Some words about my political point of view - if anybody should want to capture me - I'm a Democrat, Republican and a denier of the times religious and moralistic views - Yes, I am everything which stands in opinion to each reactionary thought. This I am of pure feeling. I would like to go back to which is natural! I would like to be a part of - active - to turn everything upside down; to be able to see what's really in the bottom. I believe that we are all too "captured"; so much ruled over; that it's impossible to do anything about it; in any other way then that it has to be burned down to the ground; be exploded into pieces - and then begin on something new!"

Quote: August Strindberg; the 29th of July 1884

Yours sincere

Leif Wilhelm

"AFTER THE AGE OF DAWN" - RÉSUMÉ OF WHAT THIS BOOK IS ALL ABOUT

Only possible here in Oslo - Norway; after then from "outside" - Namsos Wall - realize and admit what distance in evilness the generally rule of the "Namsos life" is - and that part of the so named: Namdalen is today - and the trial

against this city it self had to come - forced to come - sooner or later. And it has now already come. And I myself damn Namsos as a location on earth - the darkness continuously resting over this city in Norway - speaks in it self it clearly spoken language. "The Sodom and Gomorra shall be go through a much easier doom - and destiny - then Namsos as a town shall - be damned at "the day of dawn". Neither just without sense or reason the city Namsos as a factual case more then once almost been complete removed as a location on earth throughout history - although this location has almost not existed at all if one only look at it in a historical point of view. The Doom over this city it self will always be working - without stop or even brake - before Namsos been punished as far as possible - while the victims - both living still and dead shout from this place - begging for mercy. But there are non - in this city that even God did forget and just left - never to be there anytime. Forces will work without rest to bring the righteousness - the real content of the word in to real - and strike back again each guilty person in this area. This it self is only a natural consequence of what this district do represent to day and has done through history. And just as mercy less as the guilty ones behavior has been - just as mercy less they get their punishment. Call it a rule of nature it self if you like - that way the rule of nature do work. The shout of hurt human beings the shout and prayer of mercy and righteousness to come through - the force of nature it self - the force with end in time and no beginning of time - always there - always be

is listening - be sure of that - nothing that is unrighteouness in this world goes futhere on without being righteously punished. What this is all about it just the fact or even law of nature it self: Evilness punishes itself - nature strikes back. Both time and nature is working fore exactly the same cause - a common will and a common goal - call it chess if you like - but the last word always in this matter has nature itself. Difficult settings? Hidden meaning? Maybe so - but just watch as time passes by each word here written will confirm themselves into reality.

PROLOGUE THIS BOOK

This book about the City Namsos - the information giving is a kind of "trial and Judgment" and makes this book in it self to an end fore something that has been and after this is new way to walk forwards – the information giving in the book is interesting or as a matter of fact or even more true name of it - Yes, directly frightening informations - almost like a nightmare. One should almost not believe it is the truth being told - but although it is. Most human beings who has come from otherplaces and tried to settle in Namsos - just

leave after a very short while and just after that try to forget every thing they've experienced and just keep silent about what goes on in this city. This is the general behavior fore not so named: real Namsos citizens. I though has chosen to call what I have experience by its name - and thereby out and over with that. Shocking reading fore so called fine feeling ears and eyes - it may be so – although I only tell what I have seen and simply take the consequence of what I really have seen - and not complete alone in just this: Aage Aleksandersen also criticized very strong the living surcumstances in Namsos - and this critic true and righteous in his book release: Foreign Bird - off course this was not popular in Namsos generally among the population in the city Namsos. And in this my book release I do not mention any thing else then what concern the city Namsos - what it itself do represent - I personally do agree complete with Aage Aleksandersen in his judgment and I have seen what I have seen and make a clear - shocking maybe - but though both true and righteous judgment. This prologue and dedications are in them selves very covering of the message I want to give to the world and the books content. And now then begins the book: UNDER THE COLD STAR OF NAMSOS CITY – THE FINAL CUT:

UNDER THE COLD STAR OF NAMSOS CITY - NORWAY: "THE TRIAL AND JUDGMENT OF NAMSOS" – THE FINAL CUT

I just as nameless of so called not REAL namsos citizens, is never given the full opportunity to live in peace and freedom; as I though begged fore all the time being in Namsos town - but in spite of this it never came in to reality - although I personally achieved much in what this matter concern compared to what it mainly has been throughout the 20 years past in Namsos. But this I did achieve have cost - every inch of dignity - an ocean of suffering and almost never ending struggle concerning just the content of the word: Dignity. I myself personally as an: "Outsider" or then with other words not a real "namsos citizen" - have been terrorized in the city of Namsos fore 20 years - and then as a direct result of this very many times tried to leave Namsos and then primary to an other place in Norway. Think I have tried to move from Namsos at least five times only the last 10 years - the terror in Namsos against me then also has been extremely hard the last 10 years - between the years from September 1993 to this year in November 2003. But the "Namsos Mafia" in one way or the other forced me not to succeed in this my clear will and goal - especially using economic surcumstances - to prohobitate that I should succeed in my attempts through all these years gone - this in spite of my clear will all this time moving from Namsos and leave this place once and thereafter fore all time to be gone there from. The last time I did move - I had set a clear boarder against such activity from Namsos city to continue - I there and then all ready had more then enough of all the terror and tried very hard then in September 1998 to put an

final and thereafter eternal end to my connection with Namsos also then economically and left by airplane direction: Oslo. This was there and then my final decision and even after that time the only decision what this matter concern: "Namsos now I had enough!". But what did happen back in September 1998?! Namsos city did by force "capture" me and forced my to come back - complete unlegal. Thereafter has gone through a true "Hell" and a fight without comparation - which can't be described in detail - because to cruel to go in to each single part of it. Even one part of it to cruel to go in to describing in detail. The main criminals - guilty in this is six persons in Namsos: Olav Kristiansen, Bjorn Hildrum, Elizabeth Bratland Johannsen, Svein Ole Ystmark, Kjell Nynes and in add Kurt Moen - every one of them located in Namsos. What then at that time happen? The answer is I was forced by brutally power to live 5 years in an apartment in Namsos - against my will - I at that time had in September 1998 come to Norway's capitol: Oslo - and have since then after I was forced to come back to Namsos by these mentioned persons - and have not have had any possibility to come back to Oslo and live here as was my goal also then 5 years ago was my intention - as in due to general Norwegian law off course have the right to do so if I only wish. This sounds like an unbelievable story - but though how unbelievable it may sound it is the true in each single part of it. In a way and with full right the whole story - this part of it can be described as a "prisoning" of me as a person though then

without any legacy doing so and in an apartment in Namsos - forced against my clear expressed will not wanting it - this lasted between September 1998 until now November 2003 - unbelievable story - even in Norway as a whole complete unbelievable - but though the reality and the truth concerning this matter.

I have always and will always take fore granted and as a non-discusseable truth that: to struggle fore righteous to come through – is the life it selves deepest meaning and goal - yes, reason fore living here on earth at all - it is the only hope we the human beings in the world as a whole has the reason to living. This being the deepest truth and meaning of life on earth it self. To struggle fore righteous to come through - if there were no human being at all on earth who don't do so or didn't do so – the earth we have been given have no sense of exist or right to exist at all. Hope would in case not could have any foundation.I though know that to struggle fore righteousness - and do this without stop and always - no matter what may occur - because there are people in the world who does so is the reason that there are human beings on earth at all. If nobody at all did fight fore righteousness to come through – the life on earth would be complete meaningless. And if this the last mentioned really had been the case the earth would just had disappeared and ended up in nothing. There would be no reason to continue to keep on let the world exist - but just because this

mentioned though is not the case – in opposite to this there are really people in the world as a whole among all human being in the world it self -a human being who fought fore righteousness without stop - but he was not alone in this matter - just now there are nameless individual in the world doing just the same and there will always be. I have heard in Namsos: "You know what you have to accept!". Yes, truly I do know that - but NOT what you put in this words of content - that is to accept in your way of living and behavior - the generally accepted behavior in Namsos city - which is evelness. I in deep opposite to this know what I want to accept and that is never ever to given in fighting fore the life's deepest meaning: to fight fore RIGHTEOUSNESS to come through! And because I have seen and had just to realize that in Namsos as city generally people in Namsos do not even know what righteousness is - of this reason I can't now continue to fight fore righteousness in Namsos city - because after experience of life in Namsos throughout 20 years that I never make - my fight make any big difference not even in the long run - therefore it is meaningless to continue to fight fore righteousness to come through in Namsos as a single person. And therefore as only responsible action that make sense I have simply now taken the consequence of this factual surcumstance and simply left Namsos - once and for all time thereafter. And after this never ever again not even come near the city of Namsos nomore as long as I do live on earth.

In Namsos in add to very great part of the population generally is "working" in the so named: Social and Health Sector - "nothing doing" is a more righteous and correct name of this then the name "work".What Norway concern - and many other western countries concern - there are built up a so called: Social and Health Sector who from the start - when it all begun was meant to help people with difficulties and make life generally in this countries easier to survive in and live a life in dignity - the truth just now is though that this so called Sector has become something else - what it has become as a whole is that they shall have their "work" in this "service" - work is a complete misguiding name if their doing: "do nothing at all" is the most covering words what their so called "work" is all about. Complete no professionalism and what they all are doing the days from the start at "work" is to sit together and spread gossip and drink coffee - not anything else than just that. This phenomena incl. each part of the at its time created Social and Health Sector. The Labor Party in Norway created these institutions from the start - after world war two in 1945 - but they all has been something complete else than was the intention of creating these institutions at all. Now these institutions functions without exception in the following described manor: To be sitting at an office - have so called meetings - where nothing does happen - nothing then else to sit together and telling gossip - and coffee drinking - that's everything - and fore this they get prestigeful positions - where they have power without responsibility. And in add to

that and with this as background they are committing terror activities against weak groups in the society - these that the social and health sector - should protect. It was the reason creating these sectors at all from the start. But in add to this phenomena they are also earning large amount of money each year - paid from the country it self - each position in these sectors are costing the country itself enormous amount of money each year. These wages and in add to that coffee among the employees is everything that really is a large cost for the country each year - nothing else - believe me. I myself do really understand and complete agree with Haakon Lie - who in the age of 90 expresses with deep disappointment about what everything in this matter concern says the following: "It is nothing else then a big shame what this country - Norway - has developed it self to become and my Party: The Labor party which should fight fore with all recourses to defend those who are in a weak or undefended position in society - this party has big part of being guilty in this being the present situation that this far as ever is the case. I am deeply disappointed in this!": Quote Haakon Lie in 2002. I personally have my deepest respect and give my deepest honor to Mr. Haakon Lie - because of the human being you really are and in add a clear and true representative fore the generation: Labor Party members he do represent - and this he has been all the time during his grownup life - also during the war from 1940-45 - and the occupation of Norway at that time in history. I also do agree and am admirer of Mr. Haakon Lie in almost each point of

view he has - incl.. his clear United States Of America, United Kingdom and Israel sympathy under what ever may come - this has always been his clear line - what this matter in add concern. Never an inch of doubt where he stands concerning sympathy and thankfulness towards these nations in this world - always "Holding the Line" - a clear stand – and never reason under any sucumstances - at all to have any doubt what his point of view in the matter and feeling of gratitude and regards towards these nations - this I as an individual do admire of my whole heart.

But now over to tell about the general accepted - what the matter concern of "living" in Namsos and what Namsos really is - generally spoken and that is something really negative loaded sentence - yes, as a matter of fact even frightening in this matter concerning I even go so far to warn the population of the whole world it self - by telling that so much evelness located on one place and in a so small town almost - this I know and is my clear convention do almost not exist on earth. And this after factual watching the cold reality in Namsos throughout 20 years - more or less - last 10 years permanently living in Namsos - so I do know what I am talking about. - and in add to that I have a background to be able to compare with other places to live - especially in Norway. And here follows the doom over Namsos city - this that is my clear convention and that not ever can be left no doubt what concern this judgment - not even as much as an

inch of doubt - never allowed to have it - I have seen far enough and statement after statement - one phenomena more evel then the other - just continue that way and never have any ending. If you want to visit Hell on earth - suit your self go to Namsos - any further creating Hell on earth difficult to make in to reality - but just that they really has managed in the small town named: Namsos in the middle of Norway. And therefore is now my final conclusion and consequence I will describe in the following next part of this book -considering Namsos as living place and city: Over the City gate of Namsos - there ought to been written a warning - then the warning now following:

"The one who walks here in - there are no hope left fore.." - just as it was written over the gate to Hell in Dantes book: Inferno.

THE CONSEQUENCE I TAKEN IN MY CASE CONCERNING THE CITY: NAMSOS – NORWAY "THE FINAL CUT")

Just now and for all time – I am finally released – and gone from Namsos. And is as far as I can see the only sensible thing to do - just as Aage Aleksandersen did after the music release: "Eldorado" to leave Namsos once and for thereafter all time never to come back at any point of the life I have left on earth to live. This is just now the main thing that

have to happen - and come in to reality - every possibility has to be taken with this goal alone. What ever it may cost - to once and for all time to be released from what has been going on in Namsos all these years gone. And all this evelness can never ever be complete forgotten or forgiven - it in the long run it will punish those who were responsible in this evelness - the evelness punishes it self - it is a rule of nature itself. I have finally moved and left Namsos city once and for all time is then - now after being "prisoned" against my will to be in Namsos since September 1998 until now November 2003. I am then now finally "back to where I once belong" and then now settled in Oslo – where from I five years ago became "captured" complete without legal act of doing this - to "capture" me - and five years ago I did give a promise at the time when this clear unlegal "capturing" did take act though - I said to people I there and then came in connection with in Oslo that I would come back as fast as ever possible to Oslo. And now this happening really is factual - but that after unlegal being "captured" or if you like "prisoned" - by force to live in an apartment in Namsos - this strongly all this time against my will unbelievable but true. Lived in Stjordal from 1977 to 1982. Much of the ground foundation of my life what it has developed to and become it comes from that period of time in my life - it's beginning though in Steinkjer - between 1974 to 1976. I was born at Levanger Hospital on the 7th Of May 1960 and 3 years old - in 1963 I came to the very south of Sweden and therefrom – in an age of 14 I came back to Norway and then to the town

Steinkjer and since then I have lived my life in Norway; until now while I am 43 years old. That now just as my dear beloved brother: Werner in 1974 took me back to Norway - from an evel little village in the very south of Sweden named: Hanaskog - this place had similar phenomena as you can find in Namsos – but to become as Namsos is - is almost impossible - surely Hanaskog was a bad place for living - but compared with Namsos not anything special to talk about. Just then in Hanaskog I lived in a block - and the same has been the case the last 10 years in Namsos. I lived in Hanaskog from I was 7 years old until I was 14 years old; and now then ; just as I then left Hanaskog - I now have finally left Namsos behind and never even look back over my shoulder what this city concern. Though it became a absolute possibility that everything that had to be done to make this a reality had to be done by myself – everything that was needed. Though there also did come "angels" - that gave me help to come to the new destination. The goal is to have the possibility to live in freedom and live in freedom and peace - that really what it is all about and what the so named: "Angels" concern is it as I clearly has expressed in my life my clear and earthly convention that: "The Angels do walk on earth - it is the human beings who are flying..."

From the 22nd of November 2003 the goal was finally reached - release from Namsos to as i now has become - settled in Oslo - the capitol of Norway.

THE FINAL CUT

The name: "Namsos Mafia" - is a setting that clearly and with full righteousness I use to tell in one setting something that describe the population generally and the living surcumstances in Namsos - what kind of surcumstances. What I then do mean by this? Then I have to try to explain what the content in the word: "Mafia" is - most people know what it is - they get a feeling of something existing in the USA, though the fact is that in The USA, they are the exception - not the rule. But in Namsos it self it is completely the other way around - it is the "Namsos Mafia" who rules in Namsos it the general surcumstance. All of these so called: namsosinger cooperate as far as they can and protect each other in the purpose harm "outsiders". In this way Namsos as a city functions generally. In add to that there is a general rule i Namsos - not ever to help other human being in any case - an other rule is that if a namsosing have family he shall keep to this and not have anything to do with other persons then just they in the family. Noone visit one an other - if they do not is a part of the family. And if they have family the rule is just to keep

together with this - nothing or nobody else. And what job concern - only do this - and never ask questions about anything - no critic is accepted whatsoever. And if they get an order it is just to obey - nomatter what the orders content is - just obey and do exactly what they are told to do - never in any case think fore themselves - or take any personal responsibility at all what concern something or somebody; not even what matters them selves. If serious crimes are done because of an order the standard answer just is: "I only obeyed an order!" Isn't these words well known from history and only in one particular case as a kind of "defense". Most Norwegians know what the standard answer was for example from the Nuremberg trial against the nazis - there and then this setting where uses as a kind of "defense"! But the answer from the Trial it self - was clear and concise: "There do not even exist something like what you are saying!". "Each human being has personal responsibility in every matter what they themselves concern!". It was the answer they did get from in the trial. And this is a pure fact. Nobody are allowed to not take personal responsibility for their way of act!". It is the land of Law and Justice foundation – and it was first time in history formulate in Magna Charta in England in 1215. And Law and Justice shall always be the foundation fore each democracy complete without any exception. After the war i 1945 Norway again became a free nation - at the 8th of May 1945 - and Law and Justice as ground foundation for democracy was there and then a reality again. But what Namsos

concern as city - when you read what I tell - but I am not alone of telling this - that Law and Justice that is ruling the country Norway generally - it is definitely not the case in Namsos city. They have their own rules to follow. Especially those who come from other places and try to settle in Namsos - they clearly see the curious phenomena in this city. I myself can and that with righteous go so far that naming what this is all about to have people generally in Norway and the rest of the world to understand the most covering name is: nazism - any other word can't describe it so people understand what it is going on in Namsos. Watch - what is it going on in this town? Many so called new settlers has asked the same question - settlers as a common rule do most often just leave Namsos after a very short period of time. Normal human beings can't as a common rule live "The Namsos Life" in the long run. "The Namsos Life" as a matter of fact the same as not really living at all. Better and more true call it then death then life. To live in Namsos is as being dead. It is the conclusion I have had to take after 20 years factual watching it. And the necessary puzzle parts did really fell each into its right place and at the right time - where "Angels" came and did do their part tom make everything turn the way I deeply wanted in each detail - an the status just now the 22nd of November 2003 - the apartment in Namsos - read: "prison" - my five years long time being by force "prisoned" in the mentioned apartment in Namsos has now finally ended and I do now live in Oslo – where from I was "captured" by Namsos city five years ago

and by force - not by my own will - brought back to Namsos there and then now 5 years ago – but now then the promise I gave at that time - 5 years ago in Oslo honestly and trustworthy now finally been kept: that I would return back to Oslo. This is now then although after much more time then I thought be the case at that time. I now then hope Namsos is out of my life and never nomore have not as much as an inch with anything concerning my life - ever - but this to not let people do what they want themselves and live in freedom is just the main rule to not let people do so - it is the main rule Namsos has as a city. Lena Marianne - my dear sister - is always my heart of gold – and what me concern I will be just as my dear brother: Werner - the trustworthy - to set words on things - and call things by it's right name. In add to let a word be a word and every promise be holy - that's me - my foundation - rule to live after. In that way my dear brother Werner did function – the trustworthy - the most prominent character sign he had - and I continue to drive this heritage further on in the future and never end doing so. Sent the following SMS to my dear sister Lena Marianne: "In this land I grew up strong; taught to fight and never to give in. Now my dreams all deserted..." "Rest you're head: you worry too much – you're not the only one! You are wanted all along. Don't give up – cause you have friends. Don't give up cause I know somewhere there's a place where we do belong." Quote: Peter Gabriel. I end this part of the book now that I have done the one and only responsible just as it now has been really then especially the last ten years - five

years of clearly unlegal "prisoning" in Namsos city - I by now left Namsos city and now I do live in Oslo and I am glad fore that – I gave a promise there and then five years ago in Oslo and that was: "I will come back!" - now finally that has come in to reality; and I thereby have finally kept the promise although it took five years to make it come in to reality - there and then five years ago it was though not my intention or will that it would take so long time - but unfortunately it did. But anyhow - now finally the promise there and then given now at last kept as I from the deep of my heart did want to do. In 1974 my dear brother Werner gave me a promise and it was: "To bring me from Sweden to Norway!". And there and then just one location mentioned in Norway as part of this promise and that place was: Oslo - but at that time it though got somewhat different – it became: Steinkjer. Though now after all this time I now finally really am in Oslo and everything seems to turn out all right and now finally and then once now and for ever left Namsos city behind an never nomore set my feet in Namsos city again as long as I do live here on earth - as I also then as ending of this book give a strong warning to other human beings also not to do so - this strong warning follows now in the spelling coming here: If each human being - with human qualities - watch what really is going on in Namsos city - the common judgment - that this is a place that do not function the way that is the common - most ordinary other places. It is something that clearly is something real special - more right word courious - and in negative understanding as far

possible of this word. So is the question many people asked after watching Namsos a while: Why? The reason? Even not I can understand why or the reason. It is I am convinced complete impossible to explain - why it is this way. The only thing I can say honestly - is a warning to each ordinary - normal functioning individual: Keep away - don't ever even trawl to Namsos. Don't even come near. What happens if you go as far as settle then you can only wait for a real nightmare to start. This is my conclusion and of pure human ethical reason I give this warning. It is though the only thing I can do in this matter concerning Namsos as city - after 20 years experience with the city Namsos. "Cold - feelings" is the general that is the most common among the place even God left - so don't come to Namsos city! This is the strong and honest warning I give of pure human consideration.

One explanation of all the courious phenomena i Namsos city can have a reason in that this city as a matter of fact hasn't almost existed at all - if one only look at it in historical point of view - it has no roots – the city it self is only 150 years old. In Norway and Scandinavia generally is time what matters locations generally at least 1000 years of history – and in Scandinavia it self and Norway is proved there has been settlements as far back in tim as 10 000 years ago – as example at Stjordal is proven settlements 7000 years ago. Such things do i Namsos city and area not exist at all.1000 years ago Namsos - the whole area where

Namsos is located was under the sea - as mentioned Namsos and the city is only 150 years old. I don't know if that can explain some of the courius phenomena ruling in this town as not - far away - is the common - other places I have been and where I have lived before – even in Steinkjer - 80 km from Namsos is Egge kings house - which were over 1000 years old. Theory or thought it is – though difficult as a matter of fact to manage to explain the reason - the best thing to do I think just realize that the living surcumstances are the way they are - courious - yes - but explain - telling why - I never can understand not complete - that's the case - in the Namsos city matter as a whole.

I end this part of the book about Namsos city - and the judgment against this city - or with Roger Waters words: THE TRIAL - with a spelling that from the beginning is a text from a song made by: Bjorn Afzelius - but then made the text and title a bit different - so that it shall fit in the message I want to give and end this book with - a kind of also summarium in as few words as possible expressing my feeling and where I stand in the matter of judging Namsos City - the texts name is then: "Under The Cold Star Of Namsos City" and here it now follows:

"UNDER THE COLD STAR OF NAMSOS CITY"

(Dedicated: Linda Engelsen – though only one clear case of many - tearstained eyes)

"Under The Cold Star Of Namsos City - I saw young girls who had fallen - and blood on their clothes - where the bullets had hit them - yes, under the cold star of Namsos city I saw the same cold - mercy less terror as I remember it from Warsaw and Berlin".

With this last settings I end the mainpart of this book - and leave then with a think through.

Pure historical addition - settings following:

In Namsos as a town both grownups and children are being told to believe that the Germans during the war in 1940 were those who did attack Namsos it self by weapons. And it is a historical fact that Namsos really was one of the places in the whole of Europe who got the very most destroyed during that period of the war. The whole city it self was so to say - and factual - really complete removed - nothing left. But to tell that the Germans were those who made this a reality is not the truth. What happened though was that the Germans at that time early in April 1940 decided to have their maincourter - in Namsos in that part of Norway. This

decision it self resulted in massive attacks from the allied forces - both french and english - especially the english war ship armada was involved - and weapons used from this ships and in add bombing Namsos - the english forces did - the Germans did evacuate the civil population almost as a whole away from danger - so just a very few did loose their lives. This is the true history about the war in Namsos in 1940

LETTER TO ADVOCATE CLAS ERIC AUNE FROM ME ON 4TH OF AUGUST 2008 - NAMSOS - NORWAY - TRANSLATED FROM TWO LETTERS

To: Advocate: Clas Eric Aune - Namsos – Norway

Hello Clas Eric,

I am now moving to United Kingodom by 19th of November 2008 - and want not any of this criminal acivity by Namsos citiezenens during the time left and neither the jouney as last time three years ago now exactly it is kept in Namsos city against my free will fore three years time now last time it was fore 10 years between 1993 and 2003 - but to descriebe what did happen at that time three years ago and since then in house arrest in Namsos fore three years is following: In November 2005 when I moved direction UK - end destination the USA - was that I was attacked by a young man in Steinkjer at Railroad Station on my way to Trondheim Airport and hit by Karate - I phoned the Police -

but I was arrested instead of as natural the Karate man - I had blood all over and had starved then fore more then a month - what then happened - police hit at the door saying:

Operation - I asked what mean by that? No answer.What then happened although I had living space and my address in Trondheim and managed to get apartment fore 400 $ I was forced back by police to Namsos - and in addsince then kept in house arrest and forced to pay for it too just as much as in Oslo about 1000 $ the apartment I did have in Trondheim I lost because they forced me to stay and done now since Oct. 2006 to now Aug. 2008 and I had had to a starve a lot and been unable to manage daily survival from month to month all the time until now and just now become too much of this - clearly criminal act from Namsos authorities it is not allowed at all. None at all do so nomatter were in world. I managed in 2005 to get apparent at 400 $ in Trondheim but i Namsos forced to pay and forced to be at a payment of 1000 $ that do not make any sense - living surcumastances are not good at all - and has to be solved at once now not wait any longer - have told all about it to authorities of Namsos and have to solve this now can't continue live like this and rent must be as apartment I did get in Trondheim - been forced back now fore three years between Nov. 2005 until now Oct. 2008. But fore my sake this case must be solved now at once - not wait a day any longer can't stand that they have put me in this and has also to solve it then so get apartment at half the price of this one now in Namsos.

Please set force on Namsos Authorities in this case this to happen now.

With these words I do end this book and hope the book have given something to the one who has read it which was my intention creating this book at all.

THE END

MY LIFE AS A CHRISTIAN

By: Leif Wilhelm

I met God and Jesus 8th of July 1983 at an Airport. I became a Pentecostal Christian in 1984 - and Baptised into Pentecostal Church: Betel the 20th of September 1987 and baptized in Holy Spirit. To get Salvation from Jesus my King and Master is the biggest happening in my life and always will be. Know that the Bible is to 100% the truth - our bible not the catholic bible - but King James bible is God's words the sum of them to human kind and is Holy and the complete truth from beginning to end of the Holy Bible. THE SALVATION FROM JESUS CHRIST IS THE BIGGEST HAPPENING IN POSITIVE REMARK IN MY LIFE AS A WHOLE. I am a Christian since 8th of July 1983. I do not believe that God and Jesus exists and rules - I do KNOW it. I have met them both personally in my spirit in contact with The Holy Spirit. THE SALVATION OF 15 OF NOVEMBER 1987 THE GREATEST HAPPENING IN MY LIFE AS A WHOLE - BUT ALL HOLY SPIRITS WORK AND THEREBY JESUS WORK AND HIS IS ALL THE HONOR - HE WHO HAS ALL POWER IN HEAVEN AND ON EARTH! This book is my personal experiences about Christianity as belief but in my experience Christianity is not a belief at all – it is even written Bible itself it is the case not needed belief in whether God and Jesus is the truth it is really easy doing to get to know that not believe at all – but know. But what then belief? It is what is told: Believe in Christ and his salvation doing on other word what he himself and Bible tells is truth every setting of it – that itself is really Christian belief – really no big case to know that God and

Jesus do exist – not difficult doing at all it is – with setting I do end this spelling and this way the book itself do begin.

I do believe in Jesus Christ as my King, Master and Lord and am Pentecostal of convinsion

I was born in 1960 and the 8th of July 1983 I met Jesus and God. I know it's true: "It's only one way to salvation and that is only one name given under the Heaven that can give salvation and that is Jesus Christ and you have to speak in tongue". Jesus is the life for me. I begged a prayor 4 years old "Please Jesus let me be a tool in Your service" Only that I want to be and he uses the one who seach him. God, Jesus and Holy spirit lives in the Heart of the Christians.My deep convinsion is that the Pentecostal church is Gods only true chruch. And in add I was for many years in Pentecostal Pioneer Aage Samuelsens movement from 1983 to 1987. In 1987 Aage left fore Heaven. Just now in Pentecostal Church of Oslo. I got ordinated as a Pastor in my own Church in the USA by Senior Pastor John Carlson, USA on the 19th of August 2010 and after that been working on the web with my Church as webbased church with address in New York, NY, USA.My wife married on the 10th of September 1997 - through the Barbara Blues living in Detroit, MI, USA she also create graffity she wrote on: Bblues@hotmail.com created for "Life" she called me "Life" - thereby a marriage contract.

She is born in USA in 1970 and I look forward to 2027 20th of June when I shall move to New York, NY, USA then we shal unite she is waiting, In add I do love Norway, USA, UK,and Israel. God bless Israel, Norway, UK and USA. And love the locations Oslo, London and New York. Love the USA I do. At last God bless Israel, UK and not to forget New York and USA.

I became baptized – barried with Jesus in the baptism in Betel Pentecostal meeting 20th of September 1987 – I became clinically dead in 1983. I became clinically dead as I mention and met God and Jesus. And was of mercy given salvation and reborn on the 8th of July 1983 on Airport on my way Hospital where I should be transported to the department that healed damages I still had on the body - but had until then from the 24th of June been at a Main Hospital for operation – big operation it was and very difficult but very good doctors and they managed against all odds. – but I even became declared dead but was clinically dead – and was in the death – and met God and Jesus there among other things that did happen – saw my life as on a TV-Screen pass by at first the last that happened was that both God and Jesus were there and they said: "What shall we do with Leif?" It was said more than once. Then all of a sudden I was back to life in the hospital bed.

Singing; "HOW GREAT THOUGH ARE!" that song a praise song nothing else did fit at all none of the songs from a Agriculture Christian School did fit there and then. And got reborn and got salvation on the 8th of July 1983.

And I do know that the whole bible is God's words and it is true and to be followed and that Jesus is alive and doing that for us give us salvation – God, Jesus and Holy spirits work alone. That gods words in the Bible is the complete truth for us and that the Bible is Holy. God met me there and

Jesus at the airport the 8th of July 1983 when I said yes: "Jesus come in to my heart I want to be your child!".

And all of a sudden God's Holy Spirit filled me complete and God talked Prophetic through me for everyone who was at the airport could hear it was like thunder in the voice I was lying down to be carried in to the ambulance to take me to hospital and the quotes where from the Holy Bible:

"In the last days, God says, I will pour out my Spirit over all people, Your sons and daughters will prophesy, your young men will see visions, you old men will dream dreams. Even on my servants, both men and women. I will pour out my Spirit in those days, and they will prophesy. I will show wonders in the heaven above and signs on the earth below, blood and fire and billows smoke. The sun will be turned to darkness and the moon to blood, before the coming of the great and glorious day of the Lord. And everyone that calls the name of the Lord will be saved."

I never had read it any place - not read so much as a word from The Bible before that time.

It is written in The Holy Bible in the old Gospel but also in Acts: in Acts repeated of Peter the Rock - and it is also written that it is in the very last times that shall happen - "that God will pour out his Spirit over all people!" - and Pentecostal movement did grow up because it did happen

first time in the USA among poor people there - it was in the year of 1907 it did happen in USA – the prophesy fulfilled and it is in the end of time it shall happen it is written in The Bible. Or as Jesus Christ do say: "In the close of time!". And it will happen very soon that the end do come after that - and now 2008 - 100 years has gone since then - but still we are living in the very last days and the return of Jesus Christ were he shall judge the whole human kind - still living and those who are dead too. And divide evildoers from the righteous. But there are only one way to be named righteous and it is by take Jesus into the heart - no other way there is to salvation. Because only he is to 100% righteous - none else at all. And we are given by mercy righteousness and salvation through Jesus and Holy Spirits work alone so none have any reason to say: I am myself righteous - because none is. Except Jesus and God.

And from Isaiah in the old Gospel quote: "From now I create something new – don't you recognize it? It is already growing up.

Until then I hadn't even read in The Bible of anything of that very little as a matter of fact read in The Bible – but had had a child belief since I was 3 years old. After that I was carried in to the ambulance and got the permission to talk inside me directly to God and Jesus. And I did then say: "What is really this?" "I heard all the time: non can know God and Jesus do

exist! How then this???" Answer: "There is no problem at all knowing that we do exist everyone can know that!".

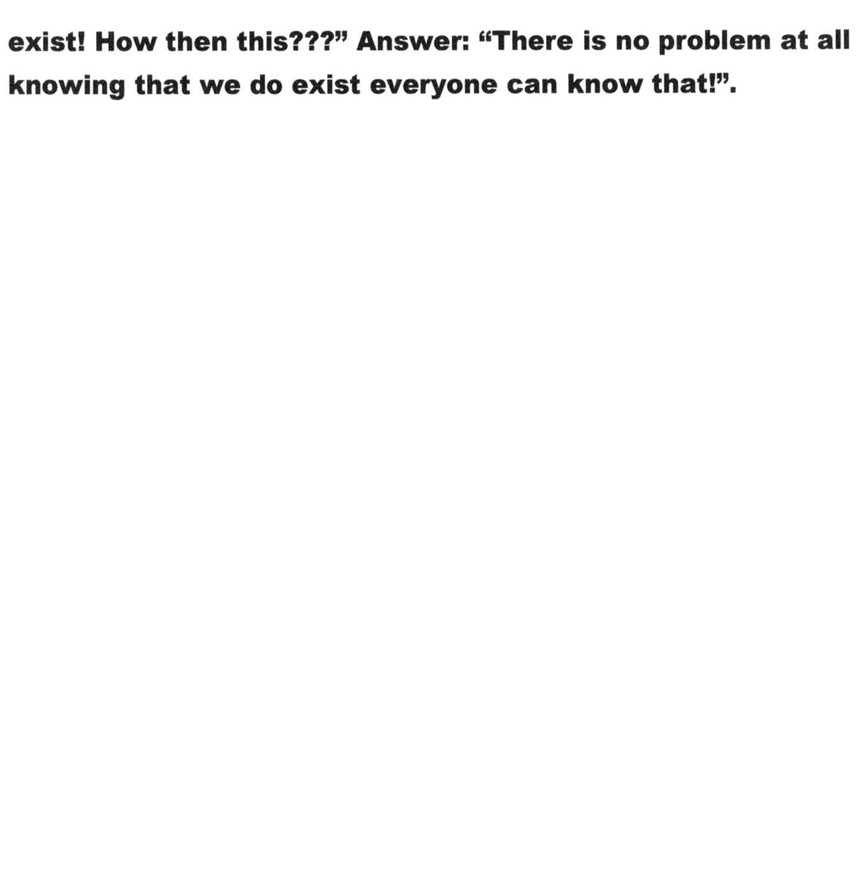

And in 1984 when I went an Agricultural School – a Christian School – to get to become an Agronomist – had gone Pure Agricultural School at first to become a farmer between 1981 and 1982 – at I went to this Agricultural School because I searched after God and Jesus. I at that time I used to go to each meeting at that School it was a Christian

School. But still not got salvation or being born again. One day early in the spring at this School I went out for a walk it was mild temperature outside and no wind at all – it was late in the evening and it was dark. Then I begged in my suffering in longing after knowing if God and Jesus is the truth. "If you are the truth then give me a sign God!" I prayed. All of a sudden in the sky just over the treetops there was lightened up a round light in yellow, I wondered – then an other one was lighten up the same way – looked like lights on a car – but up in the sky – and after that a third one; one after the other horizontally three lights in different colors – then a light was shown over that one that was in the middle: Then I thought if one in add now under the others are lightened up – it becomes a cross! all they were in different colors; and it did a fifth light was lightened up so it made a cross showing – very big could almost seems like an airplane was about to crash but the light did stand complete still and I stood watching for a long time. Then I thought maybe it is a UFO – and then I walked back to the internate – and the belief it was a UFO I did keep fore long time I had seen didn't end believing just that until 1983 8/7 – when God told: "It was a sign from me my child – you begged to me to give you one and it was given!". Is also written in bible beg and you shall be given.

In 1981 to 1984 I got anorexia but God did remove that in one day in 10th of November 1984 – after that never had it – I was only 46 kg and I am 180 cm tall and in 3 weeks I was in normal weight had to eat for three weeks and became 76 kg that is normal and God and Jesus helped my – by his wound you get healthy from sickness is also written. And 8th of July 1983 I got salvation from God and Jesus as mentioned.

When we were on an educational journey at the Agricultural School in 1985 I went to Philadelphia – a pentecostal church on meeting one day. After that because I was a youth and begun at an education: Office related and became Account Manager in 1988.

In September 1987 I had gone out of the Lutheranian Jew hateress church – this I do say because Luther has written scrips that made almost each country that had Lutheranian belief to be filled with Jew hatetress through history in Europe even used by Hitler those scripts and I wanted to become a member in the Pentecostal movement and be barried in the baptism with Jesus. Then I phoned to Betel – an other Pentecostal church and ask if they could baptize

me – complete under the water – as it is done and told in the Bible to do. And The Bible is to a 100% truth that I do know.

8th of July 1983 when from God and Jesus - they spoke through me prophetic quotes from The Holy Bible that I never before in my whole life until then had read or heard at any point. But read it afterwards.

Read much in the Bible after that time and do still do so. Know it is God's Holy word's each inch of it and the complete truth is in it to be told.

I became a personal Pentecostal Christian the 8th of July 1983 – I went baptised in the grave with Jesus Christ the 20th of September 1987 in Betel Pentecostal Church in Trondheim, Norway and came in touch as early as 1984 with Aage Samuelsen and was in his movement from then he gave me advice to join Pentecostal church of Trondheim – and 15th of November 1987 I got baptised in the Holy Spirit at Aages meeting in turnhallen Oslo and thereby was born again and got my salvation– just now I am about to join

Pentecostal movement of Norway – central in Oslo by 14th of March 2009. To meet Jesus and God and get salvation be reborn as a Christian is the biggest happening in my life and never will be otherwise – can't ever. End this spelling with these words: None comes to the Father without by Jesus!" And thank you God and Jesus the King and Lord – with all power in Heaven and on earth.

The Pentecostal Movement in Norway was started by Pastor Thomas B. Barratt with a break through in 1907. To day there is about 280 local Pentecostal churches and over 40.000 members. Thomas T. Barrat (Scottish), and Pioneer Aage Samuelsen - both with great importance even world wide fore Pentecostal church.

It was only a positive attitude and the local movement Pentecostal was blessed with the presence of the Lord himself and the Holy spirit – after being baptized in Betel I became a member at once – they did write me in at the same time as a member and that I should continue to be until 1990.

After this baptism that is urgently necessary for all human beings – there and then it came God spoke through me in Israeli language – ended with I fell on my knees saying Maran-Ata! Maran-Ata! Hallelujah! Hallelujah! The complete ending of it was :"Jesus is here, Jesus is here – Jesus from Nazareth is here." Then it ended. But the same day I was barried with Jesus in the baptism i Betel. I became then a member there the 20th of September 1987.

Pentecostal confession says that bible 100% true and I do know it is the case - I do not believe in God and Jesus I know they are the truth – and Islam most evil organization on earth and has only to be complete forbidden and removed for all time from earth before Christ do come back to judge the world - and that is in no time limit just now in July 2008. About 100 years since the mentioned prophesy was fulfilled that is written in Bible and Pentecostal movement came as direct result - and now no time limit left but Islam has to be

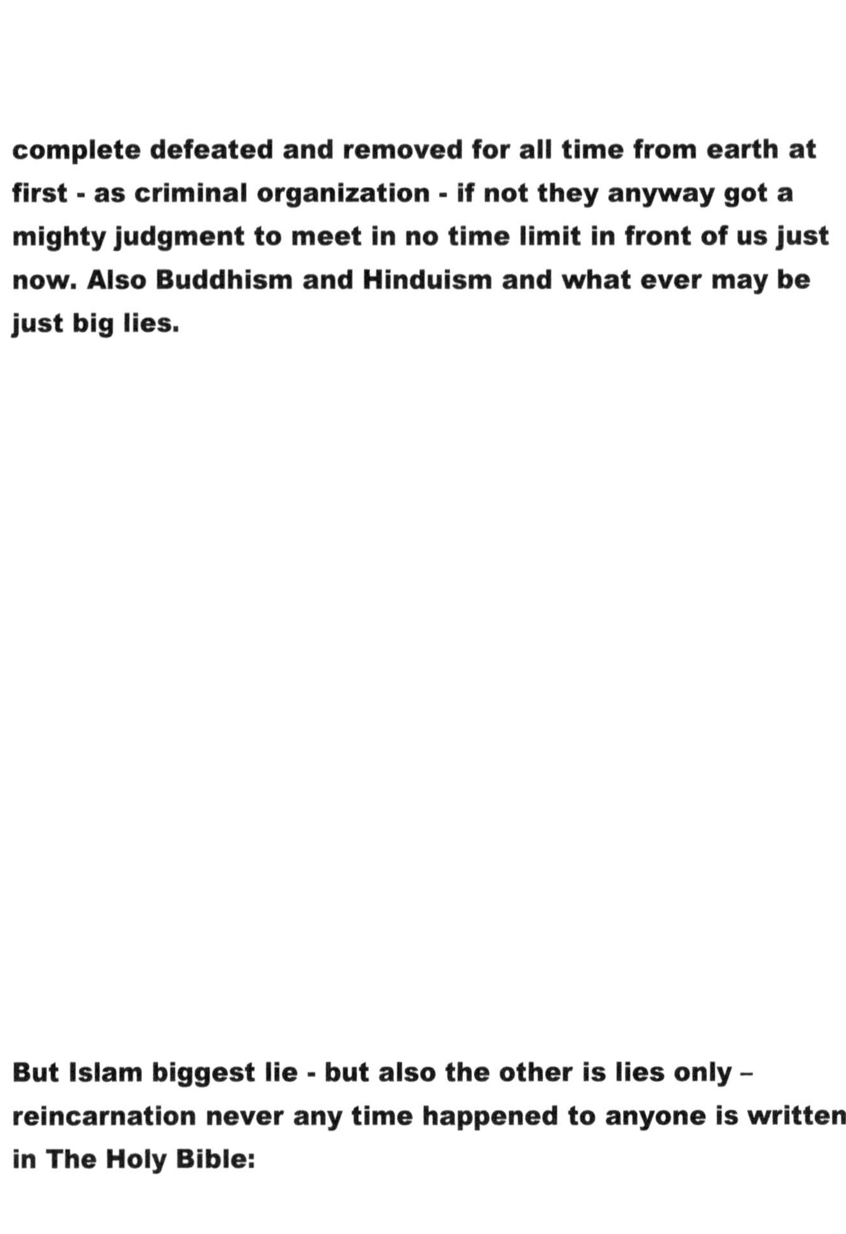

complete defeated and removed for all time from earth at first - as criminal organization - if not they anyway got a mighty judgment to meet in no time limit in front of us just now. Also Buddhism and Hinduism and what ever may be just big lies.

But Islam biggest lie - but also the other is lies only – reincarnation never any time happened to anyone is written in The Holy Bible:

"It's each human beings destiny one time to die and thereafter doom!".

And that's clearly words enough just about that matter itself. But is written also in Bible about Mohammed he is mentioned in revelation of John - Jesus disciple - as: "The false prophet to come!" - and what also Islam done - put even a Mosque in Jerusalem and written all around the socket of that Mosque: "God has no Son!" and that almost worse blaspheme ever occur and should be removed that

mosque from Jerusalem fore all time to come as fast as possible. Should been done very fast. And what happen everyone has to face Jesus after death and then be judged no matter who and two possible results of these doom then end up in Heaven of Hell - no other way is. And Jesus say himself: "None do come to the Father without through me!" - also written:

"There is no other name ever mentioned to get salvation through then God's son Jesus!".

Paul says that in Bible. And I know there are no other way for anyone no matter what has of belief on earth all meet Jesus after death - all happen to everyone no exception – no way ever to escape from that: "One time to die thereafter doom" is as mentioned written in bible and know it is true.

Islam really bad religion - as a matter of fact no religion at all - just a criminal organization - one of the biggest lies ever told – only Christianity is the complete truth - nothing else - Jesus is the truth in person himself - no matter what humans may believe there are only one real truth and this truth is Jesus Christ himself none else - this I really not believe I know it - and not difficult at all in world of today to know just that - for instance just take a look at the Corp. sheet of Torino and what is found out about it - no leave for doubt then - even Jesus said: "I shall give you only one sign after me: The Jonah Sign!" - That was in itself that he did rise from death to life and is the only King ruling and got all power in Heaven and on earth - this is the truth and Bible is truth all of it - God's words it is - spoken to humanity given them as a treasure and a gift – until Jesus do return and will judge all humankind - what Islam concern will get a very hard doom by Christ no doubt either ever to have in that matter - but we humans can even have it forbidden to exist on earth because it as organization brakes almost all of UN's declaration of human rights and that's only fact - truly they

soon gonna face reality all of them and everyone who do die cause they all are set to face Christ himself without exception... Because he has always been the only truth..

"But whoever causes the one of these little ones who believe in Me to sin, it would be better for him if a millstone were hung around his neck, and he were drowned in the depth of the sea!"

(Matthew 18,6)

I do know The Bible has the complete message to human kind from Jesus Christ himself. It is long time ago given prophesies in the Gospel Old and also in Now repeated what happened at Pentecostal time - it did come through in 1907 in The USA – it happened there first. And brought to the rest of the world - as early as in 1907.

I met God and Jesus and got salvation 8th of July and I am from that time a Christian and believe in the Bible to a hundred percent - it is written the complete truth there and believe in God and Jesus and that Jesus is King and Lord - and son of God. That be the complete truth told in Bible – Jesus do live and do rule both Heaven and earth - Jesus says himself: "Me is given all power both in Heaven and on earth and I be with you till the close of age!"

And thank you God and Jesus the King and Lord – with all power in Heaven and on earth.

God's rich blessing to the Pentecostal Movement in New York and Florida and Oslo Pentecostal Church, Norway. God and Jesus Christ be with you all and follow you wherever you may walk on the way of life – Only Jesus is the way, the whole truth and the life itself – none come to the father without by Jesus. Thanks to you all and bless you all i our in Jesus name – our Lord and King – none else has all the power and is the complete truth then Jesus and the Bible is Holy – it is God speaking in it to a 100% the Bible is truth. To meet Jesus and God and get salvation be reborn as a Christian is the biggest happening in my life and never will be otherwise – can't ever. End this spelling with these words: None comes to the Father without by Jesus!

"When the Son of man comes in his glory, and all the angels with him, then he will sit on his glorious throne. Before him will be gathered all the nations, and he will separate them one from another as a shepherd separates the sheep from the goats, and he will place the sheep at his right hand, but the goats at the left. Then the King will say to those at his right hand, "Come, O blessed of my Father, inherit the kingdom prepared for you from the foundation of the world; for I was hungry and you gave me food, I was thirsty and you gave me drink, I was a stranger and you welcomed me, I was naked and you clothed me, I was sick and you visited me, I was in prison and you came to me." Then the righteous will answer him, "Lord, when did we see the hungry and feed thee, or thirsty and give thee drink? And when did we see thee a stranger and welcome thee, or naked and clothe thee? And when did we see thee sick or in prison and visit thee?" And the King will answer them, "Truly, I say to you, as you did it to one of the least of these my brethren, you did

it to me." Then he will say to those at his left hand, "Depart from me, you cursed, into the eternal fire prepared for the devil and his angels; for I was hungry and you gave me no food, I was thirsty and you gave me no drink, I was a stranger and you did not welcome me, naked and you did not clothe me, sick and in prison and you did not visit me." Then they also will answer, "Lord, when did we see thee hungry or thirsty or a stranger or naked or sick or in prison, and did not minister to thee?" Then he will answer them, 'Truly, I say to you, as you did it not to one of the least of these, you did it not to me." And they will go away into eternal punishment, but the righteous into eternal life.

THEY IT IS GIVEN TAKES INTO THEIR HEART WHAT THE SPIRIT SAYS TO THE CHILDREN OF MANKIND

Quotes: The Holy bible.

5. July 1983 I had neardeath experiences first I felt how I left the body lying in bed at the hospital and saw my body from above then I saw my life pass as in a revue on a TV screen so nothing from any church even been to church - so I saw a tunnel with light at the end of the tunnel I went through the tunnel and there was God and Jesus and the angels asked: "What shall we do with John?" So, God decreed that I should return to life: and I woke up in the hospital bed where was full panic - and a young doctor

explained to me that I had been declared dead. When I tried to sing something but none of the songs on a Christian agricultural college that I learned passport so I sang what I could of, "How Great Thou Art!" 8th of July I was on værnes airport on the way from the hospital to Namsos Hospital and then I prayed to God and Jesus: "Dear God and Jesus let me be their children and let me henceforth become a Christian" Then answered God and Jesus immediately and God spoke prophetic through me what is written in Acts "In recent days I the Lord pour out of my Spirit upon all flesh ..." etc. had never read it and God spoke in thunder through me - since inside the ambulance, I got to speak with God and Jesus and asked them: This can then possibly be right because I have heard that no one can know that God exists to. "It is possible" they said. Yeah, so did I just accept it: I said "now that I know you're the truth do I get the answer when asking about something?" "Ask for what you want!" so they said. So I said: "There are so many directions in Christianity and now that I know that Christianity is true what should I apply that are right for you God" Then there was a delay then came the answer "Search you Aage Samuelsen!" And then I came to do so from 1984 and stands even what he stood for in 2016.

Nicodemus comes to Jesus and asks him: "How is a person saved ?!" Jesus answered, "You are scribe in Israel and do not know such a basic thing ?!" "No, Lord, I do not know it!"

answer Nicodemus. "To be saved you must be born again!" Jesus said after that "And it is by water and the Spirit" With other words to be saved you must be born again and it happens when believers baptism and Holy Spirits Baptism - that you speak in tongues or rather God through you.

Mohammed is the false prophet in John Rev and Islam his children - the devil's work. Amen

I believe in the Pentecostals message:

"Whoever believes and is baptized shall be saved" - it also follows a promise with believers baptism, the Holy Spirit baptism - and then he shall speak in tongues. That's because it happened the first time the Spirit was poured out at Pentecost among the disciples of Jesus about 2000 years ago. Baptism of children is wrong - children are innocent. "Let the little children to come unto me and forbid them not, for of such is the kingdom of heaven to": Jesus said and blessed them - but he was baptizing not them and baptism will be done by full immersion - this is clearly presented in the Bible if one just want to read . It says "We'll be buried with Jesus in baptism to stand up to the new life in Jesus Christ." "In baptism we bury the old body of Jesus." And standing up to the new life and receive Spirit baptism. Amen

"Whoever believes and is baptized shall be saved."

People ask Peter after Pentecost Fire is falling at Pentecost for about 2,000 years ago: "What shall we do now ?!"

Peter replied, "Repent and be baptized, and ye shall receive the Holy Spirit gift!". And Nicodemus one of the scribes in the Temple in Jerusalem come to Jesus under cover of night and said to Him: "I think you are the impersonation of the Christ - for no one could be on the way you are or do they works you do without being Messiah - but tell me when what will a man saved? " Jesus answered him, "You're scribe in Israel and do not know such a basic thing ?!" "No, Lord, I do not know." Replied Nicodemus - Jesus said: "To be saved you must be born again!" And further out in the chapter Jesus explains this by saying: "This is done by water and the Spirit!". And that is precisely the case must first be saved by accepting Jesus as your personal savior. Then and are baptized - go in baprizmgrave with Jesus get out the old body and resurrected to new life in Jesus Christ. And it happens act of birth anew by Spirit baptism. And one must speak in tongues. It made the first time the Spirit fell so.

And "Go into all the world and preach the gospel to all of God's creation. Whoever believes and is baptized shall be saved. But he that believeth not shall be damned. And these signs will follow those who believe: In my name shall they casting out demons, they will speak with new tongues. they shall take up serpents. and if they drink any deadly thing, it shall not hurt them; they will lay hands on the sick they shall recover "Mark: 16.15 to 18

"Whoever believes and is baptized shall be saved"

Mark 16.16

Peter was asked by the people at Pentecost after the Spirit had fallen they asked: "What shall we do now?" Peter replied, "Repent and be baptized, and ye shall receive the Holy Spirit gift." It follows a promise with baptism - and the promise is The Holy Spirit's gift. Without being believers baptized impossible first salvation, baptism and bury the old body with Jesus in baptism. And then just after you become Spirit Baptized this does not happen by yourself but that God and Jesus dwells and Holy Spirit in your heart and you must speak in tongues by Spirit baptism did the first time the

Spirit fell so. This whole is to be born again and become a new creation in Jesus Christ. ¨

Amen

I warn against Norway Party The Christians somehow Krf as silly as Bondevik devil quoting Aage Samuelsen - "The biggest devil in Norway, Kjell Magne Bondevik," end quote

Think even today expelled people of Aage Samuelsen opinions - it's an eye-opener - even God said to me after I met him in 1983 after salvation and God and Jesus spoke to me and said: "Seek you Aage Samuelsen" and so I did.

What do you say to this in from Aage Samuelsen with message directly from God in the Holy Spirit: "Beware Norway Kjell Magne Bondevik - he is the biggest devil is in

Norway!" - I mean it got its confirmation by Bondevik Government and never thought Aage anything on Krf. Never input image itself. But this first statement came on one of Aage's last meetings I had recording it - he spoke in God. Amen

Working Party in the 50s tested together with the state church and forbid prayer for the sick - said: "It went under the Medical Practitioners Law" Statskirken agreed and AP and Statskirken went to court in this trial was Aage Samuelsen who spoke all Christians cause - and won the Supreme Court upheld on any point after it is permissible to pray for the sick in Jesus' name. And in addition, Aage Samuelsen pursuant to ban a film: "Broder Gabrielsen" which should be about him and were basfermisk rather go under the blasphemy law itself the AP and Statskirken ever tried. Absolutely true is that believe it or not.

Condemned by God and Jesus is the Norwegian State Church they are with the Catholic Church the whore of Revelation. "No one has brought more to hell one of them with false teachings " Quote: Aage Samuelsen

My opinion about Aage Samuelsen strong warning for Norway against Kjell Magne Bondevik got its confirmation by the Bondevik government which was a disaster for Norway. Even Norway has not recovered from the Aage had little confidence in the AP also and they did nothing for eight years with the situation in the country after Bondevik.

God bless Pentecostal Movement in Norway:

God bless Oslo Filadelfia Church - where I have been a member since 04/20/2009 - I told my whole story for them with my relations to Aage Samuelsen and it all and they admitted me as a member God bless them plenty back for this. I was in Oslo Philadelphia as early as September 1983 it was then Terje Bertsen who spoke and it was a terrific meeting later I was in Oslo Philadelphia in July 1985 and when I was in Aage's meeting Turnhallen visited Filadelfia Oslo at noon 11.15. 1987 at 11:00 and have only positive experiences with Oslo Filadelfia and love the church. God and Jesus and the Holy Spirit bless you! Maran Ata does not want me maybe I tell too much sensational about Aage Samuelsen that I personally know - do not know. They refused me to become a member even wanted because I smoke it is irrelevant whether a smoker or not. What's going on? Only ash. Who is right I know that God was calling me to follow Aage Samuelsen and I do this day after been in close

contact with Aage Samuelsen from 1984 to 1987. And still I follow God's commandment tion to apply it Aage Samuelsen stood for and represented. Whatever. I follow when God's command still to this day in 2016 in December. Amen. Then rather than being in Maran Ata as took distance from Aage Samuelsen in his time his whole life for it even sang his songs but that was all I saw in Oslo when I van stopped by Maran Ata temple in 1986. They told me they had against Aage Samuelsen then ??? I stand then rather which I now stand in Oslo Filadelfia and they read most of the history of the main features and does not judge me.

Thomas Ball Barratt 1862-1940 founder of Pentecostals 1907

"And you in the night that watches here awaiting your groom and friend sound in the night should sound clear are you ready my friend. Soon, Jesus will come soon, Jesus will come blessed is he who is ready when Jesus comes again."

Aage Samuelsen

My experience after what God said in 1983 - 7/8 - "Seek you Aage Samuelsen of the others are all equal" - In hyclery I experienced afterwards. None was as Aage Samuelsen preaching the true gospel as will be preached. And nobody except Broder Aage does. Have searched and searched for Aage went home to God and Jesus and found it nowhere - "When the Son of Man comes will He find faith?" And somehow Abraham was one - and Noah was one existed only one who had faith: Aage Samuelsen. And he declared the whole and true gospel as will be preached. Amen

"As it was in Noah's days shall be when the Son of man coming back"

God promised me 8th of July 1983 that: "You will both go to London and New York but never Israel" I love Israel but will not be allowed by God to go there this coming of a cause that is in my background that I have sinned one once upon a time - by the time as late as July 2009 I came the first time to London - and 20th June 2027 I will move to New York. Please pray for this to be real.

Consider that Norway would become so by January 2004 budget to Bondevik devil - "Beware of Kjell Magne Bondevik Norway - he is the biggest devil is in Norway!" Quote: Aage Samuelsen 1987

Yet is not done ANYTHING with it!

Disgraceful among others what tobacco prices.

Yes, the Christmas - Aage Samuelsen was sick of it, Jesus was not born at Christmas and is a Catholic feast - I'm also sick of Christmas and all the hustle and hypocrisy around it - nothing called the Christmas story in the Holy Bible

Working Party in the 50s tested together with the state church and forbid prayer for the sick - said: "It went under the Medical Practitioners Law" Statechurch agreed and AP

and Statrchurch went to court in this trial was Aage Samuelsen who spoke all Christians cause - and won the Supreme Court upheld on any point after it is permissible to pray for the sick in Jesus' name. And in addition, Aage Samuelsen pursuant to ban a film: "Brother Gabrielsen" which should be about him and were basfermisk rather go under the blasphemy law itself the AP and Statechurch ever tried. Absolutely true is that believe it or not.

Condemned by God and Jesus is the Norwegian State Church they are with the Catholic Church the whore of Revelation. "No one has brought more to hell one them with false teachings its" Quote: Aage Samuelsen

My opinion about Aage Samuelsen strong warning for Norway against Kjell Magne Bondevik got its confirmation by the Bondevik government which was a disaster for Norway. Even Norway has not recovered from the Aage had little confidence in the AP also and they did nothing for eight years with the situation in the country after Bondevik.

I warn additionally strongly against Faith proof - it is heresy - which was founded by the false prophet: Aril Edvardsen - named as "Bugs Bassen geek in Sharon valley" by Aage Samuelsen - they are only after money and your father the devil. Likens forget Vision Norway - Vision Norway is a hypocritical moneymaker with false doctrine they go in harmony with anything and welcome those who ei should. Cf. Jn 2 letter. Amen

Aril Edvardsen like all popes no exceptions ended up in hell and burn there forever the same applies Hanevold and vision Norway. "It is easier for a camel to go through the eye of a needle than for a rich man to enter Paradise" Jesus Christ

All "Christian" hypocrisy except Pentecostalism religious hypocrisy that drives heresies and do not know the Lord Jesus Christ and not known by God and Jesus. Pharisaic hypocrisy - and those who crucified our Lord Jesus and killed all the disciples except John just - and is all the same harlot in the book of Revelation in the Holy Bible - top stands the Catholic church with the Pope all inclusive Lutheranism is sprung out of the Catholic Church . Amen

"If someone teaches you another teach an us and we got handed him be accursed" Paul the Holy Bible

Very soon now Jesus is going to return and that is the end of the end.

I will be back in my Home country USA but can't say exactly when it happens but it shall happen. I depart then directly but then it is up to you USA no other way. Longing back to my beloved USA and honor I give to USA. And Gods and Jesus blessing.

DREAM

Having a little apartment in New York - USA for the rest of my life meet Barbara Blues from Michigan again and unite.

Amen and thanks for reading this.

Very soon now Jesus is going to return and that is the end of the end.

THE END

www.ingramcontent.com/pod-product-compliance
Ingram Content Group UK Ltd.
Pitfield, Milton Keynes, MK11 3LW, UK
UKHW041919190726
13854UKWH00003B/1331

9 781365 879197